Can it fly?

Bobbie Kalman

Crabtree Publishing Company

www.crabtreebooks.com

Created by Bobbie Kalman

Author and Editor-in-Chief
Bobbie Kalman

Reading consultant
Elaine Hurst

Editors
Kathy Middleton
Crystal Sikkens

Design
Bobbie Kalman
Katherine Berti

Production coordinator and Prepress technician
Katherine Berti

Photo research
Bobbie Kalman

Photographs by Shutterstock

Library and Archives Canada Cataloguing in Publication

Kalman, Bobbie, 1947-
    Can it fly? / Bobbie Kalman.

(My world)
ISBN 978-0-7787-9502-5 (bound).--ISBN 978-0-7787-9527-8 (pbk.)

    1. Animal flight--Juvenile literature.
I. Title. II. Series: My world (St. Catharines, Ont.)

QP310.F5K34 2011   j591.5'7   C2010-901970-9

Library of Congress Cataloging-in-Publication Data

Kalman, Bobbie.
    Can it fly? / Bobbie Kalman.
       p. cm. -- (My world)
    ISBN 978-0-7787-9527-8 (pbk. : alk. paper) -- ISBN 978-0-7787-9502-5
(reinforced library binding : alk. paper)
    1. Animal flight--Juvenile literature. I. Title. II. Series.

    QP310.F5K35 2011
    591.5'7--dc22
                                              2010011296

Crabtree Publishing Company

www.crabtreebooks.com   1-800-387-7650

Printed in the U.S.A./012014/CG20131129

Published in Canada
Crabtree Publishing
616 Welland Ave.
St. Catharines, Ontario
L2M 5V6

Published in the United States
Crabtree Publishing
PMB 59051
350 Fifth Avenue, 59th Floor
New York, New York 10118

Published in the United Kingdom
Crabtree Publishing
Maritime House
Basin Road North, Hove
BN41 1WR

Published in Australia
Crabtree Publishing
3 Charles Street
Coburg North
VIC 3058

Words to know

bat   bee   beetle   butterfly

dog

duck   frog

horse   ladybug   wings

Can it fly up in the sky?
If it has **wings**, it can fly!

wings

beetle

Can a **duck** fly up in the sky?

A duck has wings,
so it can fly.

Can a **ladybug** fly up in the sky?

A ladybug has wings,
so it can fly.

Can a **butterfly** fly up in the sky?

A butterfly has wings,
so it can fly.

Can a **bat** fly up in the sky?

A bat has wings,
so it can fly.

Can a **dog** fly
up in the sky?

No, a dog cannot fly up in the sky.
It has no wings, so it cannot fly.

Activity

Which of these things
do you think can fly?

beetle

frog

bee

horse

The **beetle** and **bee** can fly.
The **frog** and **horse** cannot fly.
Do horses really have wings?

15

Objectives
- to acquaint children with animals that fly
- to understand that things that fly have wings
- to group living things that have wings
- to allow children to guess whether an animal can fly or not

Questions before reading book
"Name three animals that can fly."
"What do animals need in order to fly?"

Before reading the book, let the children know that they will be asked a question on the right-hand pages. They can then guess the answer and turn to the next page to learn if their answer is correct or not.

Questions after reading book
Which animals in the book are insects?"
(beetle, butterfly, ladybug, bee)
"Which animal in the book is a bird?"
(duck)
"Which animals are mammals?"
(bat, horse, dog)
"Which animal seems to be flying but has no wings? Is it really flying?"

Activity: Design some wings
People learned to fly by imitating birds. The first people who tried to fly attached wings to their arms and flapped them as they jumped off hills. Many years later, airplanes were invented with wings that did not flap.
Ask the children to draw some wings for animals that cannot fly, such as the horse on page 15 or the chameleon on this page. They can also draw pictures of themselves with wings.

Extensions
1. Ask the children if they have ever flown on a plane before. On a large wall map, find the places where children have flown and tape their names to those locations.
2. Ask the children if they can guess which expressions match the meanings below. Read them out one by one.
"flying colors"
"fly by the seat of your pants"
"Go fly a kite!"
(pass a test easily, do something without being prepared, tell someone to get lost)

For teacher's guide, go to www.crabtreebooks.com/teachersguides